INTRODUCTION

The ability to sight-read fluently is a most important part of your training as a violinist, whether you intend to play professionally, or simply for enjoyment. Yet the *study* of sight-reading is often badly neglected by young players and is frequently regarded as no more than a rather unpleasant side-line. If you become a *good* sight-reader you will be able to learn pieces more quickly, and play in ensembles and orchestras with confidence and assurance. Also, in grade examinations, good performance in the sight-reading test will result in useful extra marks!

Using the workbook

The purpose of this workbook is to incorporate sight-reading regularly into your practice and lessons, and to help you prepare for the sight-reading test in grade examinations. It offers you a progressive series of enjoyable and stimulating stages in which, with careful work, you should show considerable improvement from week to week.

Each stage consists of two parts: firstly, exercises which you should prepare in advance, along with a short piece with questions; and secondly, an unprepared test, to be found at the end of the book.

Your teacher will mark your work according to accuracy. Each stage carries a maximum of 50 marks and your work will be assessed as follows:

> 2 marks for each of the six questions relating to the prepared piece (total 12)
> 18 marks for the prepared piece itself.
> 20 marks for the unprepared test. (Teachers should devise a similar series of questions for the unprepared test, and take the answers into account when allocating a final mark.)

Space is given at the end of each stage for you to keep a running total of your marks as you progress. If you are scoring 40 or more each time you are doing well!

At the top of the first page in each stage you will see one or two new features to be introduced. There are then normally four different types of exercise:

1 **Rhythmic exercises** It is very important that you should be able to feel and maintain a steady beat. These exercises will help develop this ability. There are at least four ways of doing these exercises: clap or tap the lower line (the beat) while singing the upper line to 'la'; tap the lower line with your foot and clap the upper line; on a table or flat surface, tap the lower line with one hand and the upper line with the other; 'play' the lower line on a metronome and clap or tap the upper line.

2 **Melodic exercises** Fluent sight-reading depends on recognising melodic shapes at first glance. These shapes are often related to scales and arpeggios. Before you begin, always notice the *key-signature* and the notes affected by it, then work out the finger patterns on the finger board.

3 **A prepared piece with questions** You should prepare carefully both the piece and the questions, which are to help you think about and understand the piece before you play it. Put your answers in the spaces provided.

4 **An unprepared piece** Finally, your teacher will give you an *unprepared* test to be read at *sight*. Make sure you have read the *Sight-Reading Checklist* on page 17 before you begin each piece.

Remember to count throughout each piece and to keep going at a steady and even tempo. Always try to look ahead, at least to the next note or beat.

NAME		
EXAMINATION RECORD		
GRADE	DATE	MARK

TEACHER'S NAME	
TELEPHONE	

©1993 by Faber Music Ltd
First published in 1993 by Faber Music Ltd
3 Queen Square, London WC1N 3AU
Cover design by M & S Tucker
Music and text set by Silverfen Ltd
Printed in England by Halstan & Co Ltd

Improve Your Sight-reading!

Piano
pre-Grade 1 ISBN 0 571 51528 2
Grade 1 ISBN 0 571 51241 0
Grade 2 ISBN 0 571 51242 9
Grade 3 ISBN 0 571 51243 7
Grade 4 ISBN 0 571 51244 5
Grade 5 ISBN 0 571 51245 3
Grade 6 ISBN 0 571 51330 1
Grade 7 ISBN 0 571 51331 X
Grade 8 ISBN 0 571 51332 8

Violin
Grade 1 ISBN 0 571 51385 9
Grade 2 ISBN 0 571 51386 7
Grade 3 ISBN 0 571 51387 5
Grade 4 ISBN 0 571 51388 3
Grade 5 ISBN 0 571 51389 1
Grades 5-8 ISBN 0 571 51153 8
Supplementary exercises ISBN 0 571 51167 8

Viola
Grades 1-5 ISBN 0 571 51075 2

Cello
Grades 1-5 ISBN 0 571 51027 2

Double bass
Grades 1-5 ISBN 0 571 51149 X

Descant recorder
Grades 1, 2 & 3 ISBN 0 571 51373 5

Flute
Grades 1, 2 & 3 ISBN 0 571 51466 9
Grades 4 & 5 ISBN 0 571 51467 7
Grades 5-8 ISBN 0 571 51150 3

Oboe
Grades 1-5 ISBN 0 571 51026 4

Clarinet
Grades 1, 2 & 3 ISBN 0 571 51464 2
Grades 4 & 5 ISBN 0 571 51465 0
Grades 5-8 ISBN 0 571 51151 1

Saxophone
Grades 1-5 ISBN 0 571 51074 4

Bassoon
Grades 1-5 ISBN 0 571 51148 1

Horn
Grades 1-5 ISBN 0 571 51076 0

Trumpet
Grades 1-5 ISBN 0 571 50989 4
Grades 5-8 ISBN 0 571 51152 X

Trombone
Grades 1-5 ISBN 0 571 51077 9

STAGE 1 *Do*

RHYTHMIC EXERCISES

MELODIC EXERCISES

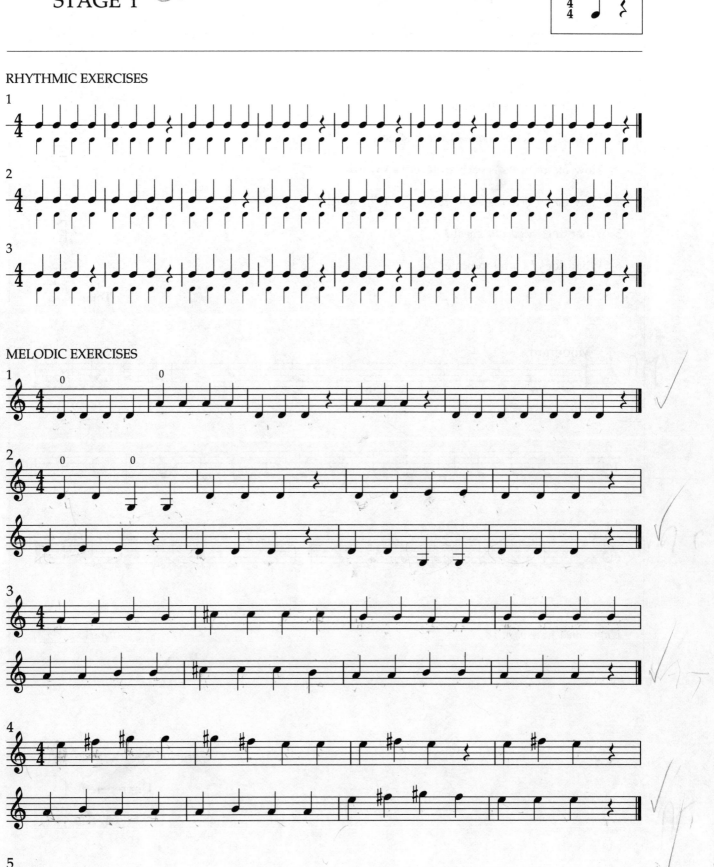

Do this page for N W (4 Oct '08)

Flora

PREPARED PIECE

Marks*

1 How many beats are there in each bar? `2`

2 What is the letter name of the first note? `2`

3 How many beats is each crotchet (♩) worth? `2`

4 How many beats is each crotchet rest (𝄽) worth? `2`

5 What does *Moderato* mean? `2`

6 What does *f (forte)* indicate? `2`

Total: `12`

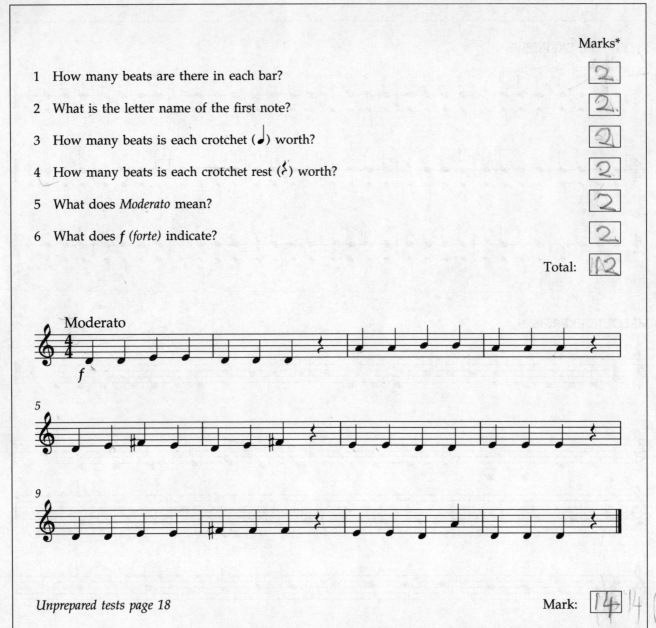

Unprepared tests page 18

Mark: `14` 14 (TN)

Prepared work total: `26`

Unprepared: `16`

Total: `42`

*The mark boxes are to be filled in by your teacher (see Introduction).

STAGE 2

19·01·04

RHYTHMIC EXERCISES

MELODIC EXERCISES

16.09.10 — scou N.W.

PREPARED PIECE

1   What does $\frac{4}{4}$ indicate? How many beats will you count in each bar?   2   2

2   How many beats is each crotchet (♩) worth?   2   2

3   How many beats is each crotchet rest (𝄽) worth?   2   2

4   What is the letter name of the first note in bar 1?
                               bar 2?
                               bar 4?   2   2

5   What does *f (forte)* indicate?   2   2

6   What is the meaning of *Allegretto*?   2   2

Total: 12   2

Unprepared tests page 19   Mark: 15   4

Prepared work total: 27   26

Unprepared: 15   5

Total: 42   41

Maddy — Feb 1st '09

Running totals:

1	2
42	42

41

STAGE 3

$\frac{3}{4}$ 𝅘𝅥𝅭

D major

RHYTHMIC EXERCISES

1

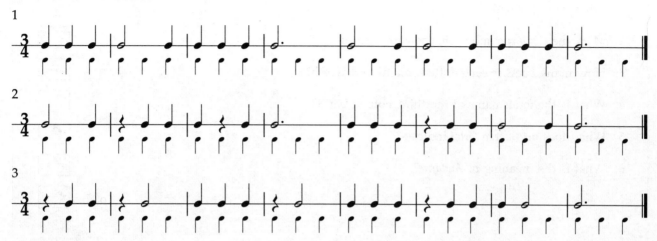

2

3

MELODIC EXERCISES

1

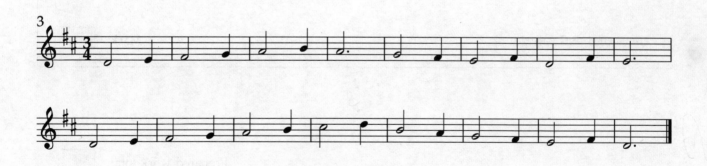

2

3

4

PREPARED PIECE

1 What does $\frac{3}{4}$ mean? 2

2 Mark the F sharps and C sharps with a cross. 2

3 How many beats is each dotted minim (♩.) worth? 2

4 What is the letter name of the third note in bar 3? 2

5 What does *mf (mezzo forte)* indicate? 2

6 What is the meaning of *Andante*? 2

Total: 12

Unprepared tests page 20 Mark: 14

Prepared work total: 26

Unprepared: 14

Total: 40

Running totals:

1	2	3
43	40	40

STAGE 4

G major
The slur + simple ties

RHYTHMIC EXERCISES

MELODIC EXERCISES

PREPARED PIECE

1 How many beats is 𝅗𝅥· worth?

2 How many beats is 𝅗𝅥 worth?

3 How many beats rest make up ▬ ?

4 What does *p (piano)* indicate?

5 What does the sign ◁ *(crescendo)* indicate?

6 What is the meaning of *Moderato*?

Total:

Moderato

p   *f*

7

p

13

f

Unprepared tests page 21

Mark:

Prepared work total:

Unprepared:

Total:

Running totals:

1	2	3	4
43	40	40	37

Oct 7th 2010

STAGE 5 Prepare for NW

RHYTHMIC EXERCISES

MELODIC EXERCISES

25·02·05

PREPARED PIECE

pianissimo

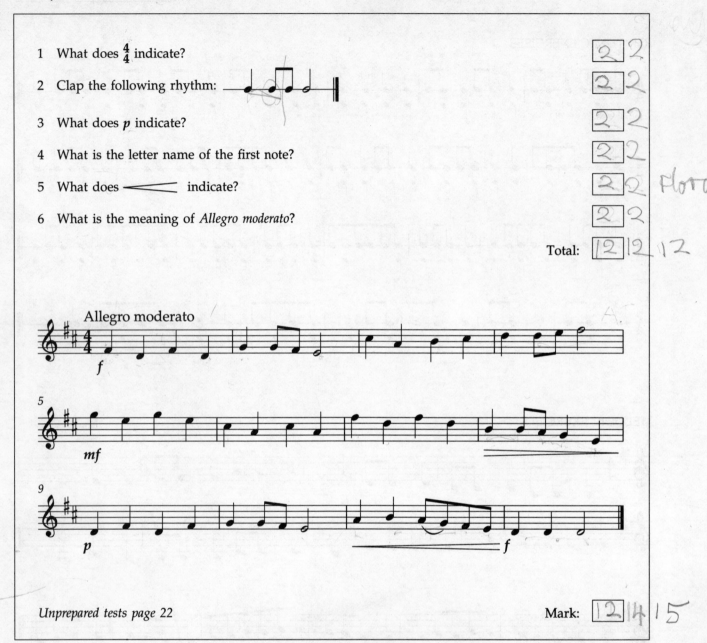

1 What does $\frac{4}{4}$ indicate? 2 2

2 Clap the following rhythm: 2 2

3 What does *p* indicate? 2 2

4 What is the letter name of the first note? 2 2

5 What does ‹ indicate? 2 2 Flora

6 What is the meaning of *Allegro moderato*? 2 2

Total: 12 12 12

Allegro moderato

f

mf

p *f*

Unprepared tests page 22 Mark: 12 14 15

Prepared work total: 24 26 27

Unprepared: 13 14 14

Total: 37 40 41

Running totals:

1	2	3	4	5
43	40	40	37	37

STAGE 6

A major

2·03·05   do just one page

say dotted!

RHYTHMIC EXERCISES

MELODIC EXERCISES

Flora

PREPARED PIECE

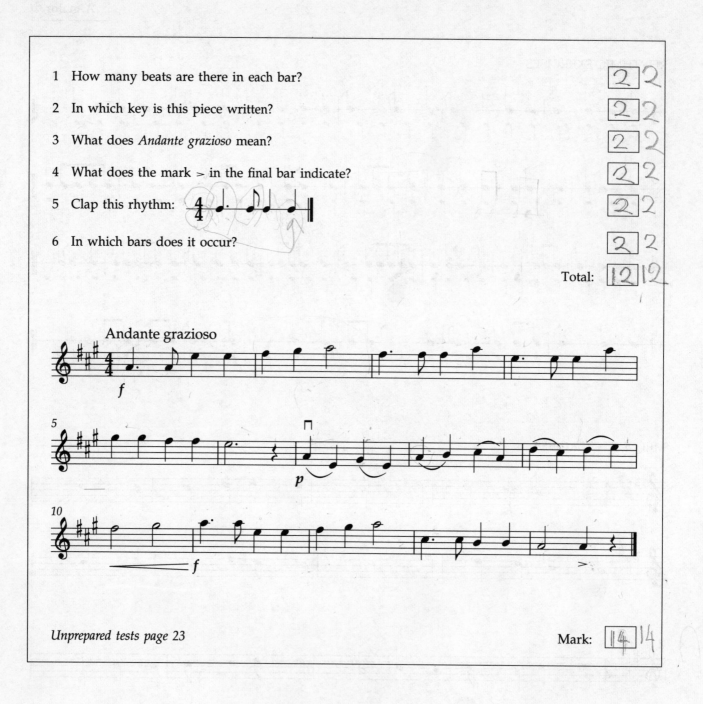

1 How many beats are there in each bar? 2 | 2

2 In which key is this piece written? 2 | 2

3 What does *Andante grazioso* mean? 2 | 2

4 What does the mark > in the final bar indicate? 2 | 2

5 Clap this rhythm: 2 | 2

6 In which bars does it occur? 2 | 2

Total: 12 | 12

Andante grazioso

Unprepared tests page 23   Mark: 14 | 14

Prepared work total: 26 | 26

Unprepared: 15 | 16

Total: 41 | 42

Running totals:

1	2	3	4	5	6
43	40	40	37	37	41

STAGE 7

> **Counting in quavers**
> $\frac{3}{8}$

Count all the work in this stage in quavers (♪).

RHYTHMIC EXERCISES

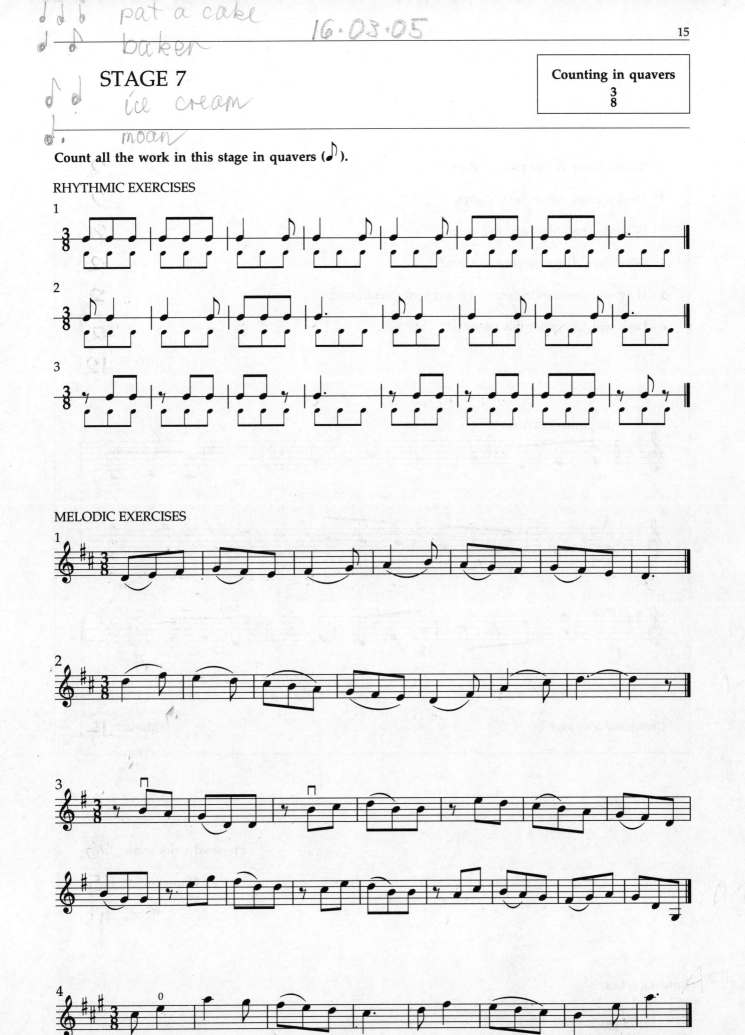

MELODIC EXERCISES

PREPARED PIECE

1   In which key is this piece written? |2|

2   Mark a cross above the C sharps. |2|

3   What do *cresc.*, *dim.* and *rall.* mean? |2|

4   What does *Allegretto grazioso* mean? |2|

5   How will the marking *grazioso* affect your performance? |2|

6   How will you count this piece? |2|

Total: |12|

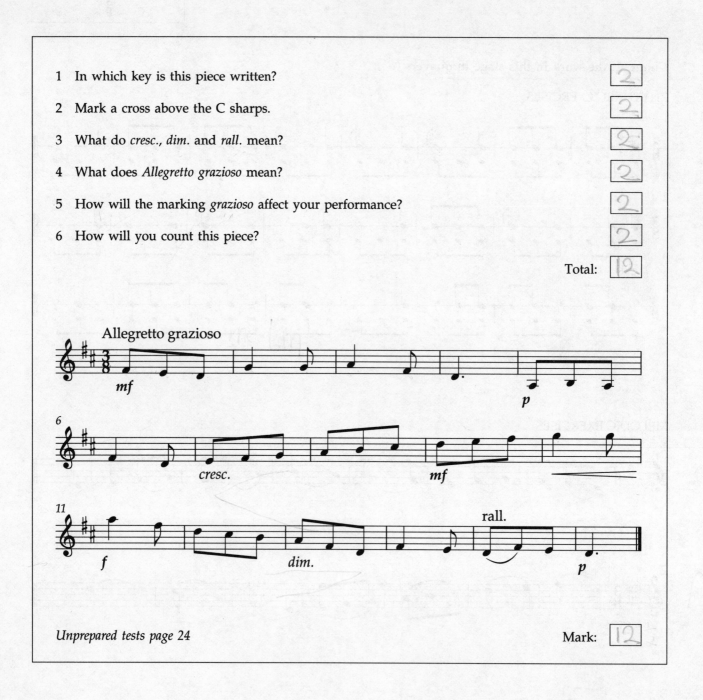

Unprepared tests page 24

Mark: |12|

Prepared work total: |24|

Unprepared: |15|

Total: |39|

Running totals:

1	2	3	4	5	6	7
43	40	40	37	37	41	39

CONCLUSION

A sight-reading checklist

Before you begin to play a piece at sight, always remember to consider the following:

1 Look at the key-signature.

2 Look at the time-signature, and decide how you will count the piece.

3 Notice any accidentals that may occur.

4 Notice any scale and arpeggio patterns.

5 Notice dynamic levels and other markings.

6 Look at the tempo mark and decide what speed to play.

7 Count one bar before you begin, to establish the speed.

When performing your sight-reading piece, always remember to:

1 CONTINUE TO COUNT THROUGHOUT THE PIECE.

2 Keep going at a steady and even tempo.

3 Ignore mistakes.

4 Check the key-signature at the beginning of each new line.

5 Look ahead – at least to the next note.

6 Play *musically*.

UNPREPARED TESTS
STAGE 1

1 Andante

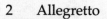

2 Allegretto

3 Moderato

STAGE 2

1 Moderato

2 Allegretto

3 Allegretto

STAGE 3

1 Allegretto

2 Andante con moto

3 Moderato, tempo di valse

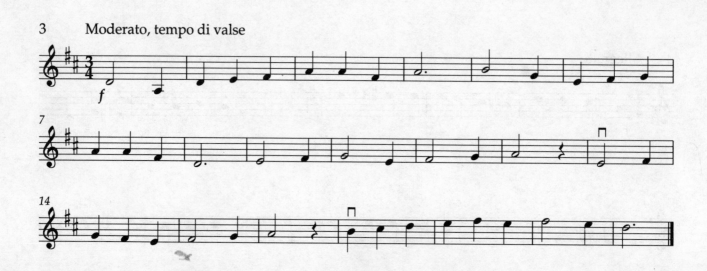

STAGE 4

STAGE 5

1 Moderato

2 Allegretto grazioso

3 Allegro moderato

STAGE 6

1   Allegretto

2   Moderato

3   Tempo di valse

STAGE 7

1   Andante espressivo

2   Moderato con moto

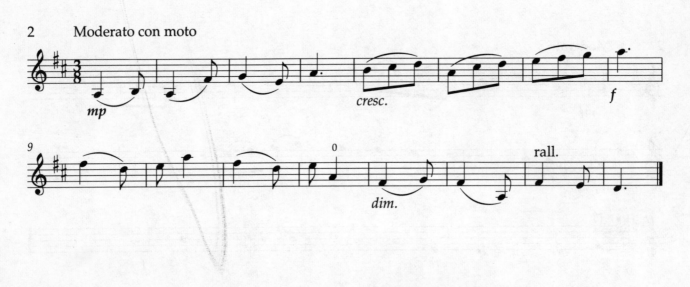

3   Allegro ritmico